TIE-DYE!

EASY INSTRUCTIONS FOR 20 FANTASTIC PROJECTS

KATHRYN KREIDER

CB
CONTEMPORARY
BOOKS
CHICAGO · NEW YORK

Library of Congress Cataloging-in-Publication Data

Kreider, Kathryn, 1950–
     Tie-dye! : easy instructions for 20 fantastic projects / by
Kathryn Kreider.
         p.   cm.
     Bibliography: p.
     ISBN 0-8092-4374-1 : $11.95 (est.)
     1. Tie-dyeing.   I. Title.
TT853.5.K74   1989
746.6'64—dc19   89-471
                                       CIP

Published by Contemporary Books, Inc.
180 North Michigan Avenue, Chicago, Illinois 60601
Manufactured in the United States of America
Library of Congress Catalog Card Number: 89-471
International Standard Book Number: 0-8092-4374-1

Published simultaneously in Canada by Beaverbooks, Ltd.
195 Allstate Parkway, Valleywood Business Park
Markham, Ontario L3R 4T8 Canada

CONTENTS

ACKNOWLEDGMENTS

A special thanks to those who provided essential assistance: Susan Buntrock, my editor, for the right idea at the right time; Betsy Blumenthal and Jean Reichenbach for proofreading; Peter Harrington of Farquhar International for dye technology and Dylon Dyes; Lisen and Lauren Reichenbach, Kelsey Kreider, Betsy, Dana, and Greg Blumenthal, Ellen Kreider, Katherine Wirick, Jeanne Tyler, and Cheryl Kosovski for research and development; James Kreider for computer technology; Elizabeth Wilson for access to her Japanese textile library; Lu Duerkson and Linda Ligon for encouragement; and Elinor and Gerald Kreider for their gifts.

INTRODUCTION

With the renewed interest in tie-dye, there is a need for a book that includes the new dyes and new approaches to tie-dye. This book unlocks the secrets of tie-dye and decodes the mysteries of using dye for new dyers and for those who, after several years' hiatus, are getting back to dyeing.

Experimenting with dye and dye colors is half the fun of tie-dyeing. The results are exciting because they are always unpredictable. Although the instructions included in this book are designed to give specific answers to tie-dye design questions, the purpose of this book is to inspire you on to future challenging dyeing experiments.

Tie-dye is defined as folding and binding fabric before immersing it in a dye pot. The areas that are bound resist the dye, patterning the fabric. With the recently introduced technique for painting dyes directly onto the fabric, this definition has been expanded. This innovative process yields a similar yet more vibrant effect than traditional immersion tie-dye. The instructions in this book are the result of experimentation based on traditional ways of tie-dyeing. These instructions are not hard and fast rules, nor are they exact duplication of past techniques. They are designed to give you ample room to experiment with your own ideas once you learn the basics.

There are a great many variations of tie-dye. Resists can be made through tying, knotting, binding, stitching, folding, and clamping. The fabric can be folded, twisted, or crumpled in either a meticulous or random manner. The dye can be applied by either soaking the resisted fabric in the dye bath or by pouring or painting the dye on specific areas. You can remove the color from fabric that has previously been dyed by bleaching and then adding new color to the discharged areas. Predyed fabric can be overdyed, adding new colors as well as patterns.

The craft of tie-dye has changed dramatically over the past twenty years. Patterns are much more sophisticated and intricate. Developments in dye chemistry and technology have changed the way dyes are used. Highly sophisticated resist dyeing from Africa and Asia has set a new standard for quality. The number of fiber artists exhibiting resist dyeing has brought a new appreciation for craftsmanship and study of traditional techniques.

Before we begin, a short history of tie-dye is in order. Using dyes to embellish the body or decorate garments dates back to prehistoric times. Nearly every culture in the world developed or learned dye technology. With increasing complexity and sophistication in dye methods came experimentation with the use of the dye to pattern as well as color the fabric.

The earliest known example of tie-dye is from Peru, from the Paracas textiles of the first or second century B.C. In Japan, tie-dyed fabrics have been found that date from the seventh century. Tie-dye can still be readily found throughout India, Africa, Japan, Southeast Asia, China, the Middle East, and certain areas of Central Asia.

In the United States, tie-dye has come in and gone out of fashion several times. First popular in the 1920s, tie-dye experienced its greatest resurgence in the 1960s, when it became a symbol of the counterculture. It has been suggested that the technique was brought to the United States by returning Peace Corps volunteers who had served in Africa and Asia and had learned the craft from their hosts. A contributing factor to the success of tie-dye during that era was that fiber-reactive dyes, which were easy to use and colorfast, had just become readily available.

Grateful Dead fans have been perhaps the strongest influence in keeping tie-dye alive since the 1960s. Tie-dye T-shirts are ever-present at their concerts, with independent entrepreneurs vending creative, dazzling products. Now, the teenagers of the 1960s are the parents of teenagers. Having raised their children on rock and roll, both generations look back to the 1960s as a golden age, with tie-dye as one of its most symbolic elements.

The recent resurgence of tie-dye has many roots and sources, making it difficult to document historically. The current American fashion scene is an eclectic assimilation of diverse fashion tastes. Today, there are many businesses manufacturing or importing fabric from Central and South America, Asia, and Africa. Clothing made from these fabrics are appearing in small boutiques as well as department stores all across the country. And now, with this book, you can make your own fashion statement by creating dazzling works of tie-dye art.

CAUTION

Read and follow all directions carefully. Use dye in a well-ventilated area. Avoid direct inhalation of dye dust. As with all chemicals, keep away from small children. In case of eye contact, flush eyes with water. If swallowed, drink milk or water and call a physician immediately. Reactive dyes are reactive chemicals and occasional cases of respiratory allergy have occurred among persons who have handled them.

1
WHERE TO BEGIN

Included with this book are three tinlets of dye and two packets of fixer. You have one tinlet each of red, yellow, and blue dye. These are the basic primary colors from which you can mix a multitude of other colors. If you are not familiar with color mixing, read the section on color mixing in Chapter 2 before you begin. The projects also include information on color mixing.

With the three tinlets of dye, you will have enough dye solution to make three T-shirts using one of the three methods of tie-dye:

presoaking, direct application, and immersion. After you have learned the basics of tie-dye, you will want to purchase more dye and try the other examples in the book. A complete resource list is included in Appendix C.

Be sure to read the safety precautions in Chapter 3. Dyes are chemical substances and need to be handled with care.

There are three basic approaches to tie-dye. All three methods begin by folding or gathering the fabric and binding the bundle tightly with string or rubber bands. The folds and the binding prevent the dye from reaching the fabric inside the bundle, so some areas will remain undyed while other areas readily take up the dye.

You can follow any of the three methods listed below. They all yield wonderful results. For the first three tie-dye projects in this book, Method 1 was used.

TIE-DYE METHODS
1. Presoaking

The fabric or clothing is soaked in a solution of fixer and salt. The dye is dripped, painted, or sprayed onto the damp fabric, which has been folded, crimped, clamped, or laid flat. The dyed fabric is kept damp for at least 24 hours. The excess dye is then rinsed out. The longer the dyed fabric remains damp, the brighter the colors. The fabric can sit for several days for more brilliant colors.

2. Direct application

The chemical fixer is dissolved in the liquid dye and the dye is painted, printed, or sprayed directly onto the flat or folded fabric. The fabric can either be dried and then heat-set or it can be kept damp for 24 hours. Then the excess dye is rinsed out.

3. Immersion dyeing

The fabric is folded and tied very tightly with string or rubber bands. The fabric is then immersed in a bucket containing dye, chemical fixer, and water for a specified length of time. Then the fabric is removed, the bindings are taken off, and the fabric is rinsed to remove excess dye.

The first two methods are recent developments and employ the direct-application technique of dyeing. Direct application is painting, dripping, or otherwise applying dye directly onto the fabric.

WHAT CAN BE DYED

The dye included with this book is called *fiber-reactive dye*. This is the dye most commonly used by fiber artists for tie-dye and other dye techniques. Fiber-reactive dyes are very light- and wash-fast, and they easily give pale to brilliant colors.

Fiber-reactive dyes work only with natural fibers such as:

- Cotton
- Raffia
- Rayon
- Linen
- Wool
- Silk
- Jute
- Ramie
- Sisal
- Hemp
- Other animal fibers

Fiber-reactive dyes will not dye synthetic or man-made fibers, which are primarily products of petrochemical derivatives and are not easily dyed. If you want to dye synthetic fibers, you will need to use a dye designed for synthetics. Most of these dyes are difficult to use and the fumes are noxious. Most dyers prefer to use fiber-reactive dyes and to dye completely natural fibers.

If your clothing or fabric is a blend of a natural fiber and a synthetic fiber, you can use fiber-reactive dyes, but the dyed colors may be pale and the colors will tend toward the heather tones. Keep this in mind when you are purchasing shirts or fabrics to be dyed. Look for 100 percent cotton for the best results.

Should you have fabric that is of unknown fiber content, you can easily identify the fiber using either a *crush test* or a simple *burn test* (see "Fiber Identification" on page 8).

FIBER IDENTIFICATION

If you have a fabric with an unknown fiber content and you want to dye it with fiber-reactive dyes, there are two very simple tests that can aid the fiber identification, since fiber-reactive dyes can dye only natural fibers.

Cellulose fibers are from plants and include cotton, linen, jute, and ramie. Rayon is regenerated cellulose and is considered a natural fiber. Protein fibers are the hair or excretions from animals and include wool, mohair, alpaca, angora, and silk.

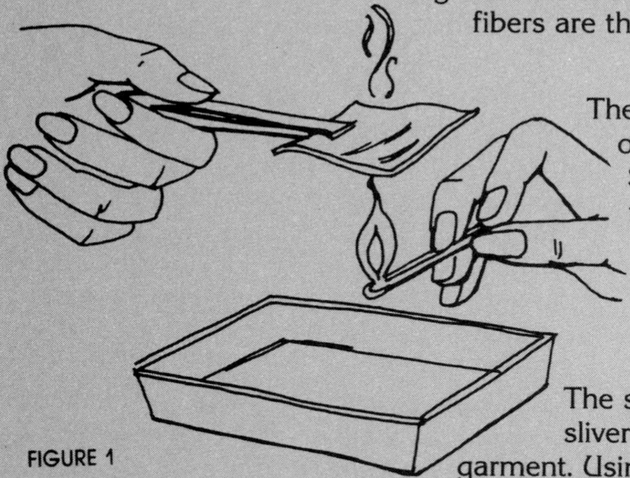

The first test is the *crush test*. Take a small point of fabric and twist it tightly into a sharp pigtail. Squeeze the point for 5 seconds. Gently undo the twist. If the cloth is quite wrinkled and the wrinkles are hard creases, then the fabric may be a natural fabric. If the twist smooths out with few or no remaining wrinkles, then the fabric is probably a synthetic.

The second test is the *burn test*. Cut a 1-by-¼-inch sliver of fabric from the seam or inside hem of the garment. Using scissors, tweezers, or pliers, hold the fabric

FIGURE 1

over an ashtray or sink. Ignite the fabric with a match or lighter (Figure 1). Do not blow out the flame; let the whole sample burn. Observe the way the fabric burns: whether it self-extinguishes, what sort of ash or residue remains, and whether the smoke and ash have a smell. Compare your results with the following chart.

FIBER	BURNING	RESIDUE	ODOR
Cotton and cellulose	Ignites easily, burns rapidly	Gray, feathery ash that can be crushed	Burning paper
Wool, silk, protein	Difficult to ignite, sputters as it burns, self-extinguishes	Black, crushable bead	Burning hair or feathers
Synthetics, acrylics, polyester	Ignites easily, burns rapidly with big flame, melts	Black, hard bead, difficult to crush	Slightly acrid or chemical

FIGURE 2

EQUIPMENT

The equipment required for tie-dye is minimal. Most of what you need can be found around the house:

- Jars for mixing and storing dye (Figure 2). Each jar should hold at least 1 cup and have a wide mouth. Peanut butter or olive jars work best. You will need one jar for each dye color plus extra jars and cups for mixing dyes to obtain additional colors.
- Teaspoon and measuring cup for mixing the dye. Several additional plastic spoons for stirring and applying the dye are useful.
- Dish-washing gloves to protect your hands from being stained.
- Dye pots for immersion dyeing, presoaking the fabrics, and washing the dyed fabric. These can be plastic buckets or dishpans, but they must hold enough water to cover the fabric. Do not use zinc or tin containers

because they will darken the dye colors.

- Tools for applying the dye (Figure 3). These include paintbrushes, cotton swabs, squeeze bottles, empty hair-spray bottles that have been thoroughly washed, syringes, spoons, ear syringes, eyedroppers, and pipettes.
- Plastic drop cloth or large plastic bags to protect the work areas. Dyes can stain wood, some tiles, bricks, older Formica, and fiberglass.
- Bindings to hold folded or gathered fabric. This includes anything that is strong and will resist the dye, such as string, rubber bands, elastic thread, quarter-inch elastic, C-clamps, tire inner tubes cut in bands, strips of polyester fabric, twist ties from garbage bags, plastic bags cut into strips, box string from an Asian grocery, telephone wire—virtually anything you can find.

FIGURE 3

FIGURE 4

2
PREPARING THE DYES

Materials and equipment you will need to prepare the dye solution (Figure 4):

- 3 wide-mouth jars that hold 1 cup of water
- 3 plastic spoons
- Dish-washing gloves
- 1-cup measure
- Dust mask

First, dissolve your dye powder in water as follows: Carefully empty one tinlet of dye into a jar. Fill the measuring cup with ½ cup warm water (Figure 5). Add about 1 tablespoon of this water to the dye powder (Figure 6), stirring to make a thick paste, much like making a white sauce. (Note: always add water to the dye powder; do not add dye powder to water, as this will allow the dye powder to float. The dye will not dissolve easily and will be lumpy.) Add more water, ⅛ cup at a time, stirring thoroughly until the entire ½ cup of water has been added to the dye (Figure 7). The dye should be completely dissolved with no lumps. Mix

FIGURE 5

the most brilliant shades. They can be stored for several weeks in a cool dark place and will still retain their potency. One-half cup of stock solution is sufficient to dye one shirt a very intense shade or three to four shirts a medium shade.

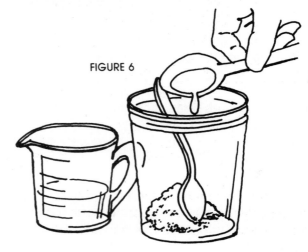

FIGURE 6

the other two colors in the same manner.

You have made very concentrated dye solutions, called *stock solutions*. Stock solutions can be diluted with water to make pastel shades or can be used full strength for

FIGURE 7

To mix the same solution if you have bought dye in a larger quantity, use 1 level teaspoon of powdered dye for each ½ cup of water.

PRINCIPLES OF COLOR

Dyes can be mixed like paint to achieve a broad spectrum of colors. Because dyes are chemical substances, the combination of colors is not always predictable, but dye mixing does follow the basic principles of color mixing.

There is a specific vocabulary for discussing color. *Hue* is the term for the color itself. Red, orange, and violet describe hue. *Value* is the darkness or lightness of a hue. *Intensity* is the brightness or dullness of a hue. Since there is no white dye, pale colors, or hues with a light value, are made by using only a small amount of dye. Dark colors are created by using large amounts of dye and by adding a small amount of black to a hue. The lightest value of red would be pink; the darkest red would be burgundy. The most intense hue is the dye in its pure,

MEASURING AND MIXING DYES INDOORS

The primary problem with measuring dye indoors is that the dye powders are easily airborne. Dye dust can quickly disperse throughout a drafty room, settling on people, furniture, and flat surfaces. Not only is this messy to clean up, but dyes can cause an allergic reaction in some people. If you must measure dye indoors, the following procedure is recommended:

1. Place a 5-gallon bucket, large dye pot, or cardboard box on its side in the sink or bathtub; this will be the measuring chamber. Cover nearby surfaces with newspaper. Lightly spray the paper with water. Airborne dye that settles on the paper will cling to it.

2. Place measuring spoons, mixing cups, dye containers, and a cup of water inside the measuring chamber.

3. Wearing dish-washing gloves and a dust mask, measure the first amount of dye into its mixing container. Add 1 or 2 tablespoons of water. Stir until the dye is a paste. Set aside.

4. Continue to measure the other dye colors, mixing each into a paste before going on to the next.

5. Gradually add ½ cup water to each dye color, stirring thoroughly. By measuring and initially pasting the dye while inside the mixing container, much of the airborne dye can be kept in check.

6. Rinse the measuring bucket or dye pot. If a cardboard box was used, place in a trash bag and dispose.

undiluted form. To dull a color, or reduce its intensity, the *complement*, or opposite hue on the color wheel, is added to the pure color.

The *primary* colors are red, yellow, and blue. They are called the primary colors because combinations of these three colors yield all other colors. The primary colors are pure hues; no other colors can be mixed together to create a primary color. If red and yellow are mixed in approximately equal parts, they produce orange. Blue and yellow produce green, and red and blue produce purple. Orange, green, and purple are called *secondary* colors.

If a primary color is mixed with a secondary color, the resulting color is called a *tertiary* color. Red mixed with orange yields red-orange. Yellow mixed with orange yields

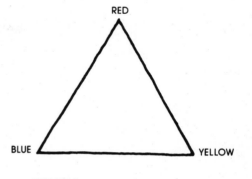

FIGURE 8

yellow-orange and so on.

The best way to understand color is to visualize a color triangle with the primary colors, red, yellow, and blue, at each point of the triangle (Figure 8). Midway between each

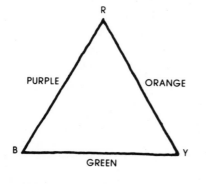

FIGURE 9

secondary and tertiary colors produces a circle, or wheel, which depicts the relationships of the colors (Figure 11).

The color wheel depicts other color relationships that are useful for designing color combinations. The colors opposite on the color wheel are called complements. Blue point are the secondary colors, orange, green, and purple (Figure 9). The six tertiary colors, red-orange, yellow-orange, red-violet, blue-violet, blue-green, and yellow-green, are midway between the primary and secondary colors (Figure 10). Placing the primary colors on the triangle and then inserting the

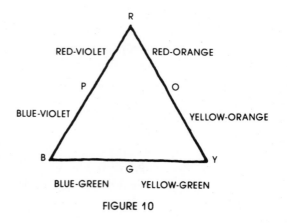

FIGURE 10

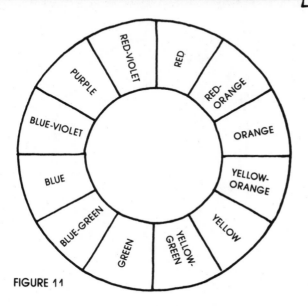

FIGURE 11

the same shirt is vivid and dazzling. But if the dyes commingle and overlap, they yield brown.

Colors that are side by side on the color wheel are called *analogous* colors and will always harmonize. Blue-violet, blue, and blue-

and orange, red and green, and yellow and purple are the standard complements (Figure 12). A pair of complementary colors used in

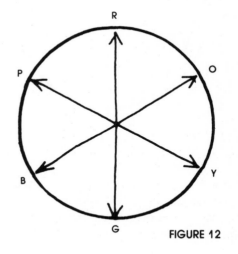

FIGURE 12

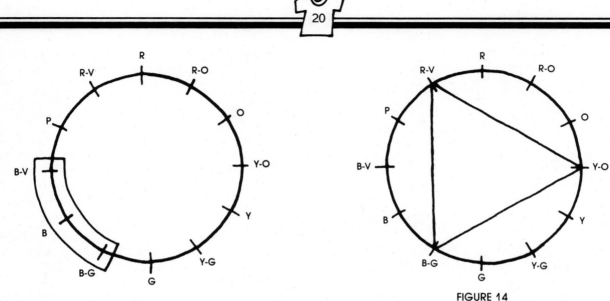

FIGURE 13

FIGURE 14

green are analogous (Figure 13). Equidistant color groups are also considered harmonious. Blue-green, yellow-orange, and red-violet make a triad, or equidistant

triangle, of harmonious colors (Figure 14). Red, blue-violet, green, and yellow-orange are equidistant, making a square in a more complex yet harmonious relationship (Figure

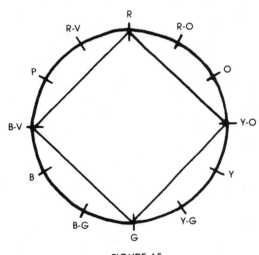

FIGURE 15

15). You will want to experiment with colors and color mixing to find your favorites.

For further information on color and color relationships see the Bibliography for books on color.

COLOR AND FIBER-REACTIVE DYES

There are many different kinds of reds, yellows, and blues in fiber-reactive dyes. The dye suppliers have different names for the various colors; some suppliers carry only a few colors, others carry dozens. The differences in hues are the result of the chemical structure of the dye. If the same blue were mixed with two different reds of different values, the result would be two completely different purples. Experimentation teaches the most about color mixing with fiber-reactive dyes. The following list may help in choosing dyes.

- **Reds**
  True Red is a mixture of scarlet and fuschia
  Fire Engine Red, or Camelia Red, is a
      bluish red and yields better purples

Chinese Red, or Mexican Red, is a yellowish red and yields better oranges
Scarlet produces better oranges
Fuschia produces better purples

- **Blues**

  True Blue is a mixture of 1 part fuschia to 4 parts turquoise
  Turquoise produces brighter purples and greens
  Navy, or Midnight Blue, produces deeper purples and forest greens
  Indigo is a mixture of 4 parts navy to 1 part turquoise

- **Yellows**

  Lemon Yellow, or Primrose, produces brighter greens
  Golden Yellow produces rich oranges

- **Black**

  True, dark black is difficult to achieve with any dyestuff, and fiber-reactive dye is no exception. Generally, more dye is required to reach black. With normal amounts of dye, charcoal gray is the usual result. Black can be the most interesting dye to use for direct application since black dye is a mixture of all the primary colors. The colors used to mix black have different absorption rates, so an area painted with black may be haloed by another color that wicks (or runs) away from the black.

3
DYE TECHNIQUES

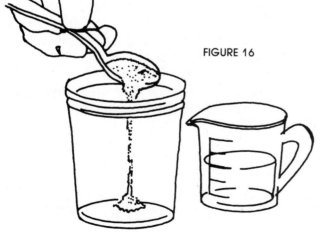

FIGURE 16

Although dye is easiest to handle in liquid form, it is manufactured and sold in powdered form. As a powder, dye has a longer shelf life, is lighter and easier to ship, and is more convenient to store. A dye stock solution is a concentrate made of dye particles dissolved in water. For tie-dye, a stock solution made of 1 teaspoon of dye powder to ½ cup of water (Figure 16) is sufficiently strong to give vibrant colors without an excessive amount of dye washing off. A stronger stock solution will waste dye

WORKING SAFELY WITH DYES

It is important to keep in mind that you are handling industrial chemicals when you use dyes. You should use dyes in a responsible manner to protect yourself, those around you, and your environment. Some people can be allergic to dyes. Those who are prone to other allergic reactions should proceed with extra caution. The primary hazard of dyes and their chemical assistants is inhaling the particles and fumes.

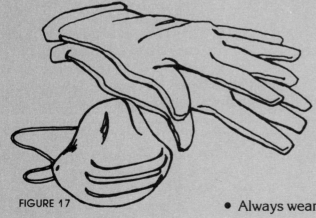

FIGURE 17

You should follow these safety guidelines when working with dye:

• Mix the dye into a liquid form to make it easier to apply and to prevent the dye particles from floating around your work space. In order to avoid inhaling the powders when you mix the dye, wear a dust or pollution mask (Figure 4). Work outdoors if possible to prevent contaminating inside surfaces with floating dye powder.

• Always wear rubber gloves when handling the powdered or

wet dye and the fixer. One of the most easily dyed substances is your own skin. Surgical or dish-washing gloves give the most flexibility (Figure 17).

- Wear clothing that is protective or can be dye spattered.
- DO NOT bleach your hands if they have become stained with dye. Bleach is too strong for your skin. If your hands are stained, scrub with a hand cleanser and a nail brush. The color will disappear on its own in 24 hours or so.
- Never eat, smoke, or drink in the dye room since this may cause you to ingest particles of dye that are floating in the air. The primary hazard of dyes is irritation from inhaling the dye powders and the fixer, sodium carbonate.
- Avoid wearing contact lenses when handling the dye powders and fixer, which could abrade your eyes or lenses.
- Do not use the same containers and utensils for dyeing that you use for cooking. Keep a separate set of dye pots, stir rods, and measuring spoons for dyeing.
- Cover work surfaces with newspapers or plastic sheeting when you are dyeing indoors. If you spill dye on your countertops, a liquid or powder countertop cleanser will remove any stains.
- Do not measure or mix dyes near furnace or air conditioning vents. Dye powders are quite light and easily airborne.
- When working with children, always use the dye in liquid form.
- Do not use dyes in any form if you are pregnant or think you may be pregnant.

because the fiber can take up only a certain amount of dye. Any extra dye will not adhere to the fiber and will be washed away in the rinses.

As was discussed in Chapter 1, there are three basic approaches to applying fiber-reactive dye when tie-dyeing. The presoak method is demonstrated in the first three projects; direct-application and immersion dyeing follow the projects.

PRESOAK METHOD

After soaking the fabric in fixer, the dyes can be applied to specific areas of the damp fabric. This allows a more painterly approach to tie-dye. The fabric can be folded, gathered, or spread out flat. The dye can be poured, sprayed, painted, or dripped on in designs. The dyed fabric should remain damp for 24 hours so that the dye can affix to the fiber.

The fabric can be rinsed earlier, after 8 hours, but the colors will not be as bright. For the most brilliant colors, the damp fabric should sit for up to 3 days.

FIGURE 18

Materials and equipment you will need to mix the presoak solution (Figure 18):

- 3 adult-size large T-shirts
- 1 large bucket or dishpan

- ¾ cup salt (¼ cup per shirt)
- 2 packets of fixer
- 1-cup measuring cup
- 1 plastic drop cloth or 3 large garbage bags
- 1 spoon

Procedure for Presoak Dyeing

Materials and equipment you will need for presoak dyeing (Figure 19):

- Dye stock solution (already mixed, see page 13-15)
- Tools for applying the dye: ear syringe, eyedropper, etc.
- Rubber bands or heavy string for binding
- 4 pencils
- 6 small plastic cups for mixing secondary colors of dye
- 1 pair of dish-washing gloves

FIGURE 19

1. Wash new shirts to remove any sizing.

2. Prepare the presoak. Pour 2 gallons of water into a large dishpan or plastic bucket. Carefully empty both packets of fixer included with this book into your

FIGURE 20

presoak dishpan. Add ¾ cup of salt (Figure 20). This can be regular table salt or noniodized canning and pickling salt.

3. Stir the presoak solution to completely dissolve the salt and fixer. Put three T-shirts into the presoak and let stand for at least 30 minutes, making sure the shirts

are completely covered by the presoak solution.

4. Mix ½ cup of dye stock solution from each tinlet of dye (see page 13).

5. Spread a plastic drop cloth or several large plastic bags over your work area.

6. After the shirts have soaked for at least 30 minutes, wring them out so they are just damp.

7. Fold and dye the shirts using the techniques described in the following sections.

8. Rinse the shirts using the method described in the next section.

Rinsing

The shirts should sit in a plastic bag to keep the dye moist for at least 24 hours to help the dye affix to the fiber. For the most brilliant colors, they can sit for up to 3 days.

Rinsing should be done by hand to prevent excess dye from contaminating nondyed areas. Rinse one shirt at a time. Rinse each shirt quickly, so the dye from one color area does not contaminate another color area. Beginning at one end of the shirt, rinse about one third of the shirt with warm water until the rinse water is nearly clear. Squeeze the shirt to remove the dye. Rinse the center third and then the upper third in the same manner. Remove the bindings. Rinse the whole shirt. When the excess dye is removed and the rinse water is nearly clear, place the shirt into a soap soak.

Using about ½ teaspoon of liquid dishwashing soap, fill a bucket with the hottest tap water possible. Place the first shirt in this solution while you go back and rinse the second and then third shirt as above and place each in its own soap soak. The hot water and soap draw out excess dye that has not reacted with the fabric.

After all three shirts have been in the soap soak for at least 10 minutes, rinse each until the water runs clear. If the soap soak is dark and dye filled, do another soap soak. Rinse again until the water runs clear.

Lay the shirts flat to dry. Avoid hanging them to dry, as there may still be small particles of excess dye in the shirts that can wick down and blur your color areas.

Diagonal Accordion Fold

Spread a damp shirt out flat on a clean section of your work area. Fold the shirt in half on a diagonal line that extends from the lower left corner to the upper corner of the right sleeve (Figure 21). From this diagonal line, accordion fold in 1-inch increments to

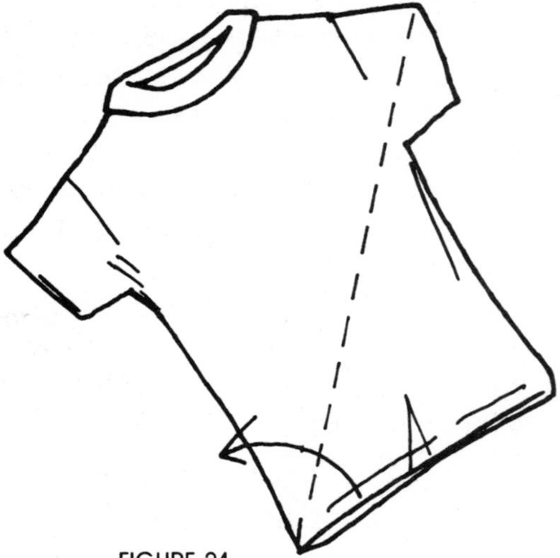

FIGURE 21

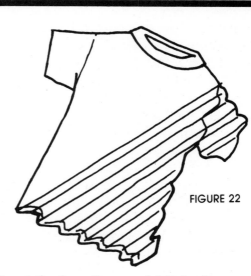

FIGURE 22

the lower right corner (Figure 22). Gently turn the bundle over and fold the other diagonal half in accordion folds to the upper corner of the left sleeve (Figure 23).

Stand the bundle on a folded edge, so folds are on the top and bottom and the flat areas are on each side (Figure 24). Squeeze gently to tighten the folds. Bind with several rubber bands.

Fill the syringe, eyedropper, or ear syringe

with any one of the colors of stock solution. Carefully apply this color of dye along each fold line. Squeeze out enough dye so it seeps down about ½ inch. You will use about ¼ cup of dye for this (Figure 25). When there is no white remaining on the edges, gently turn the whole bundle over so the other folded edges show. They should still be white.

Using another mixing cup, mix ⅛ cup of dye from each of the two colors you have not used to create a new, mixed color.

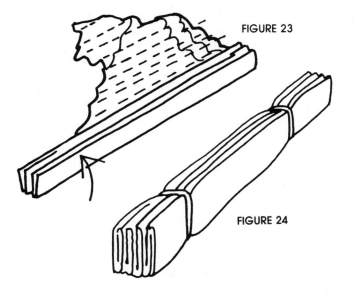

FIGURE 23

FIGURE 24

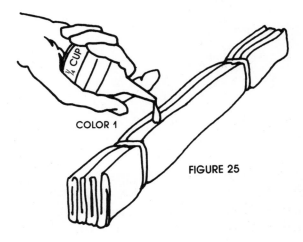

COLOR 1

FIGURE 25

Apply dye to the folded edges of this side of the bundle as follows: Visually divide the bundle into thirds, lengthwise. Apply the mixed color to the center third, one of the unmixed colors to the lower third, and the other unmixed color to the upper third (Figure 26). You will use a total of ¼ cup or less of dye on this side. There may be some

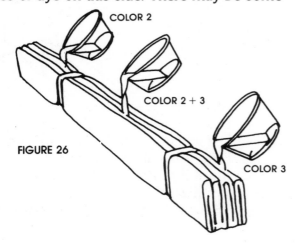

COLOR 2

COLOR 2 + 3

COLOR 3

FIGURE 26

FIGURE 27

white fabric remaining. The white areas will make the shirt more dazzling (Figure 27).

Gently slide the shirt into a plastic bag to sit for 24 hours until the time for rinsing.

Japanese Paper Fold (Flag Fold)

Lay the damp shirt out flat on your clean work surface. Smooth out the wrinkles. Fold in half, lengthwise, so the sleeves match (Figure 28).

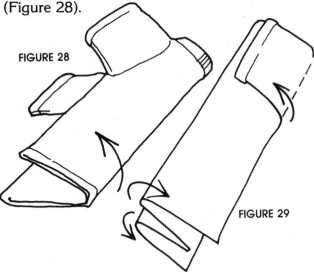

FIGURE 28

FIGURE 29

Fold back one side on the quarter line; fold the sleeve up. Turn the shirt over and fold back on the quarter line of the other side. Fold that sleeve up (Figure 29). Straighten so the piece is a long, narrow band.

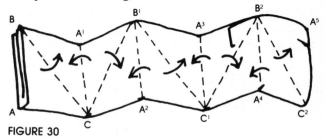

FIGURE 30

The following fold is similar to folding a flag for storage. Starting from the hem (Figure 30), fold Point A to Point A^1 on line BC. Fold Point B backward on line CA^1, matching Point B to Point B^1. Fold forward on line CB^1, matching Point A^1 to A^2. Continue in this manner, folding forward and backward to make a compact triangular bundle.

Your triangular bundle has two equal sides and a longer base. Place two pencils on top of the bundle parallel to each other and

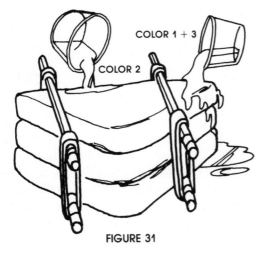

COLOR 1 + 3

COLOR 2

FIGURE 31

vertical to the base, dividing the triangle in thirds. Place two more pencils under the bundle directly below the first two pencils. Using four rubber bands, bind the ends of the pencils together (Figure 31). These pencil clamps will act as a resist.

As you did for the first shirt, mix ⅛ cup of any two of your three stock solutions to form a new color. Paint this color all the way down the points of the T-shirt triangle, so the dye permeates an inch in from the points. Paint the side edges of the triangle with any of the remaining primary colors. Leave at least ⅛ cup of each dye stock solution for the third shirt.

Place the shirt in a plastic bag to sit for 24 hours until the time for rinsing. (See Figure 32 for completed shirt.)

FIGURE 32

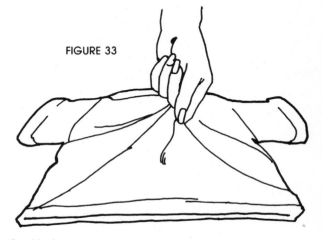

FIGURE 33

Spiral

Lay the damp shirt out flat on your work surface. Select a point slightly below the sleeves, near the center of the body. Pinch this point and lift the shirt (Figure 33). Smooth it away from this point. Holding the point, grasp the lower edge of the wedge and twist the whole shirt tightly until the shirt starts to spiral around itself (Figure 34). Continue twisting and roll the shirt into a doughnut, with the point at the center. Stretch a rubber band around the outside perimeter.

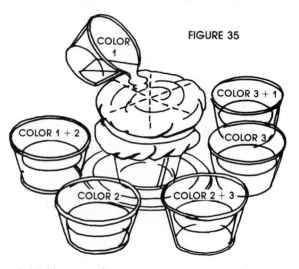

FIGURE 35

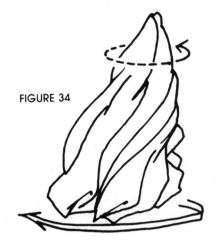

FIGURE 34

Add ⅛ cup of water to each container of pure dye and mixed color. Prop the twisted shirt on a flat side on an extra mixing cup in the center of the disposable plastic plate. Excess dye and water will drain from the shirt as you apply the dye colors. Slowly apply each dye solution in five or six pie-shaped wedges of color (Figure 35). The slower you apply the dye, the more dye will soak into the

FIGURE 36

center of the bundle. Use half of the remaining dye. Turn the doughnut over and paint the other side to match the color of the wedges to the first side.

Place the shirt in a plastic bag to sit for 24 hours, until the time for rinsing. (See Figure 36 for completed shirt.)

DIRECT APPLICATION OF DYES

Materials and equipment for direct-application dyeing (Figure 37):

- Dye stock solution
- Additional cups for mixing other dye colors
- Several plastic spoons
- Tools for direct application: spray bottles, syringes, paintbrush, silk screen, rubber stamps, sponge, etc.
- Fixer (4 teaspoons per ½ cup stock solution)

- Dish-washing gloves
- Drop cloth or large plastic garbage bags
- 6 plastic spoons
- Bindings: string, rubber bands, etc.

Fiber-reactive dye can be applied directly to fabric by painting, screen printing, spraying,

FIGURE 37

sponging, stamping, etc. In the direct-application method, the fixer is added to the dye before it is applied to the fabric. As in the presoak method, the dyed fabric is kept damp for 24 hours to set the dye.

Screen printing, painting, and stamping require that the dye be thickened with sodium alginate, a seaweed-derived thickening agent, so the colors do not bleed together. For tie-dye, the thickener is not necessary unless very crisp, sharp lines are desired.

Mix the dye in the standard proportions— 1 teaspoon of dye to ½ cup water (see mixing instructions, pages 13-15). Add 4 teaspoons of sodium carbonate fixer to the stock solution (Figure 38). Stir thoroughly, making sure all the fixer is dissolved. Dye that has been mixed with the fixer will bond to the hydrogen molecules in the water, so the dye will retain its reactivity for only 4 hours. After that, the dye is no longer functional and should be thrown out.

Fold and bind the shirt or fabric to be dyed (see Figures 21 to 35). Using a paintbrush, syringe, spoon, or squeeze bottle, apply the dye. Squeeze the fabric on the dyed areas in order to force the dye into interior folds. Turning the fabric over, apply the dye on the underside, forcing the dye into the fabric. Place the fabric in a plastic bag to sit for 24 hours before rinsing. See pages 28-29 for rinsing instructions.

For additional design possibilities, spray the dye on the fabric. Use a hair-spray bottle that has been thoroughly rinsed out. Dissolve the fixer in the dye stock solution and fill the hair-spray bottles with dye. Lay the fabric or shirt flat on a large piece of plastic to catch excess dye and the overspray. Spray directly onto the fabric. For patterns or images, lay

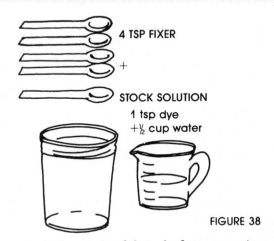

4 TSP FIXER

+

STOCK SOLUTION

1 tsp dye
+½ cup water

FIGURE 38

paper stencils on the fabric before spraying (Figure 39).

If the fabric is dripping with dye, lay it flat in a large plastic bag to sit for 24 hours before washing. If the fabric is only damp with dye, it can be rolled in plastic for the setting period. Do not fold dyed areas onto each other because they will bleed.

FIGURE 39

IMMERSION DYEING

Immersion dyeing is the traditional method of dyeing fabric a solid color. Smooth, evenly dyed fabric is easily accomplished with fiber-reactive dyes in a room-temperature dye bath. First, a dye pot is filled with a specific quantity of warm water and a measured amount of dye and salt. The fabric is immersed in the dye bath for 15 minutes, removed while the fixer is added, and then returned to the dye bath to complete the chemical reaction.

The amount of dye in relation to the weight or quantity of fibers to be dyed determines the brightness of color. The more dye used for a specific amount of fiber, the more vivid the color. Less dye yields paler colors. There is a maximum amount of dye that the fiber can take up. At a certain point, no matter how much dye is used, the color will be no brighter.

An adult-size T-shirt weighs approximately 100 grams (3.5 ounces). One teaspoon of dye powder yields the darkest color on an adult-size T-shirt. For paler colors use less dye.

If you are dyeing several T-shirts, use 1

teaspoon of dye powder for each shirt. If you are dyeing other items besides T-shirts, use the following figures as guidelines for choosing how much dye you will need. The approximate weight for 1 square yard of muslin-weight fabric or one T-shirt is 100 grams; a standard pillow case is 150 grams; a bed sheet is 700 grams.

Procedure for Immersion Dyeing

Equipment and materials (Figure 40):

- Bucket or dishpan to hold at least 2 gallons water
- Dish-washing gloves
- Plastic teaspoon, measuring cup, or wide-mouth jar
- Regular or iodized salt (¼ cup for each 100 grams fiber)
- Fiber-reactive dye (1 teaspoon for each 100 grams fiber)

FIGURE 40

- Fixer (sodium carbonate) (4 teaspoons for each 100 grams fiber)
- Liquid dish-washing soap

Wash and dry new fabric or shirts to remove sizing. Fold and bind in the chosen tie-dye pattern (see Figures 21 to 35), being certain to tie the bindings very tightly.

Figure the quantity of dye necessary, using

1 tinlet of dye or 1 teaspoon for each shirt, or 100 grams of fiber. Measure the dye into a measuring cup or wide-mouth jar. Add 1 tablespoon of warm water and stir to make a paste with no lumps. If the dye does not mix in easily, add a few drops of liquid dish-washing soap to help the dye dissolve.

When the paste is smooth, gradually add ½ cup of water, ⅛ cup at a time. Stir to completely dissolve the dye before adding more water.

To prepare the dye bath, pour 3 quarts of water per T-shirt into the dye pan. Add ¼ cup of salt for each shirt. Stir to dissolve the salt.

Carefully pour the dye stock solution into the dye bath, using water from the dye bath to rinse the mixing cup and spoon. Stir.

Immerse the tied shirts and fabric in the dye bath. Stir gently for 15 minutes.

Remove the shirts and fabric from the dye bath. Add 1 packet of fixer or 4 teaspoons of sodium carbonate for each shirt or yard of fabric.

Return the shirts to the dye bath. Stir occasionally for the next 30 minutes.

Remove the fabrics from the dye bath. Rinse in warm water, squeezing out the excess dye. When the water is nearly clear, remove the bindings. Rinse again until the water is nearly clear.

Using about ½ teaspoon of liquid dish-washing soap, fill a bucket with the hottest tap water possible. Immerse the shirts in this solution for at least 10 minutes. The hot water and soap draw out excess dye that did not react with the fabric.

Rinse again until the water runs clear. Wring out excess water. Lay flat to dry. Do not hang while damp because there may still be small particles of excess dye in the fiber that can wick (or run) down the fabric and darken the color at the bottom.

4
MORE RESIST PATTERNS

Tie-dye was probably developed by dyers using indigo dye, a *vat dye*. Vat dyes are a class of dye with a chemical composition that is very different from fiber-reactive dyes. Vat dyes are insoluble in water, so they must be treated with a reducing agent such as lye (sodium hydrosulfite) in an alkaline environment. Basically, the dye is oxygen starved. When the fabric is immersed in the dye solution, the indigo moves into the fiber. When the fabric is removed from the solution, the oxygen in the air reaches the indigo and causes it to change back into an insoluble pigment within the fiber.

It was quite easy to prepare resists with indigo because even simple folds in the fabric would prevent the oxygen from reaching the soluble indigo and changing it back to the pigment. Binding the fabric to prevent the oxygen from entering became an important design technique.

Fiber-reactive dyes cannot use the added element of oxygen deprivation for effective dye resists. However, similar results can be achieved by using very tight bindings that do not allow the dye to seep into the fabric. There are many different folds and resists that have been developed. They can be categorized by the technique that produces a specific pattern. The techniques are:

- Texture patterns:
    crushing or marbling
    overall twisting, and spiral twist
    knotting
    stitching and crimping
- Specific-shape patterns:
    circles, dots, and points
    stripes
    squares

TEXTURE PATTERNS
Crushing

Crushing, or marbling, is the easiest, quickest method to achieve a textured pattern on fabric. The image, depending on the fabric used, will appear crystalline or cloudlike (Figure 41).

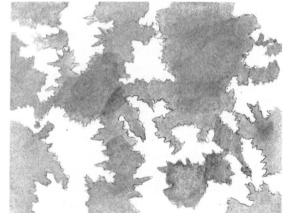

FIGURE 41

Gather the fabric into a bundle by crushing it in small tucks and folds, keeping the right side of the fabric to the outside (Figure 42). Bind by wrapping elastic or string around the bundle in various directions until it forms a solid mass (Figure 43). The binding should be very tight. Both the folds and the bindings will resist the dye.

Dye the bundle by the immersion method (see Chapter 3). The outside of the bundle will absorb more dye than the inside. With careful crushing, the pattern can be controlled.

After the fabric has been dyed, washed, and dried, the technique can be repeated to build up weblike layers of different colors. Recrush and tie the fabric so areas that received less dye are on the surface. If the fabric is dried between dyeings, the dye lines will be crisper. Crushed fabric patterns can also be used in combination with any of the other tie-dye patterns.

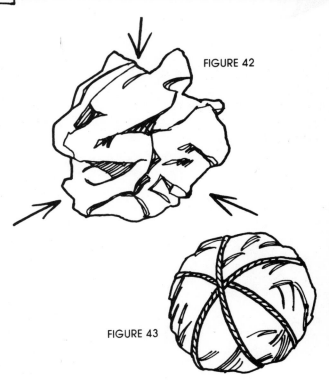

FIGURE 42

FIGURE 43

FIGURE 44

Overall Twisting

Another overall texture pattern can be made by twisting the shirt or fabric before it is bound (Figure 44). Bunch the top and bottom edges of the fabric to make a rope (Figure 45). Twist in one direction (Figure 46) until there is so much spin in the fabric that when you bring the ends together, the fabric coils back on itself and countertwists into a fat cord (Figure 47). Bind the ends together and then bind the rest of the coil. The bindings and the twists will provide the resist when it is immersion dyed.

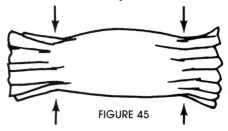

FIGURE 45

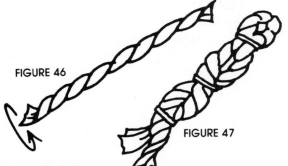

FIGURE 46

FIGURE 47

Spiral Twist

The spiral twist can be an energized design. Choose a point in the center of the shirt, slightly below the armholes. Pick up the shirt at that point, smoothing the fabric away from the point. Grasping the bottom of the shirt, twist the shirt until the spin is so tight the shirt shapes into a doughnut with the point of the shirt in the center. Put a string or heavy rubber band around the outside perimeter of

the doughnut. Dye either by immersion or by painting the dyes on in triangular wedges in either the direct application or presoak process (see Figures 33 to 36).

Knotting

An easy way to produce texture is to tie knots into the fabric. Finer-weight fabrics work best, but T-shirts can be tied into knots. The whole fabric can be bunched into a cord, twisted slightly, and then knotted (Figure 48), or individual points can be selected and small knots tied at these points. A piece of fabric is easier to knot lengthwise.

FIGURE 48

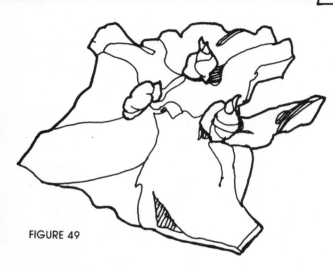

FIGURE 49

points to be tied with a pencil or tailor's chalk. Grasp one point and smooth the fabric away from the point. Twist the point until it is small enough to twist around on itself and tie into a knot (Figure 49). The knots are difficult to untie when the fabric is wet. Use a crochet hook to pry the knots loose.

Stitching and Crimping

Stitching and crimping is a variation of the Japanese resist technique known as *bomaki*, a dyeing process in which the fabric is wrapped around a large wooden pole, bound, and compressed. This variation involves stitching the fabric into narrow tubes, and inserting PVC or plumbing pipes into the tubes to achieve a similar resist effect.

PVC pipe is available in various diameters, from ½ inch to 6 inches. Cut the PVC pipe into 24-inch lengths; sand off any rough edges.

For a T-shirt, bunch the shoulders in one hand and the tail in the other, stretching slightly. Twist once or twice, and tie as many simple, overhand knots as possible.

To tie individual points, use a lightweight fabric, such as a handkerchief. Mark the

Pin two identical pieces of fabric together, or spread out a prewashed and dried T-shirt. With tailor's chalk, draw parallel lines on the fabric; the distance between the lines will be determined by the sizes of PVC pipe. The lines need to be close enough to make tight-fitting sleeves for the pipes. The lines do not need to be straight, only parallel. On the shirt, stitch from one opening to another, that is, from the armhole to the hem or from the neck to the hem. Sew all the lines before inserting the pipes (Figure 50).

Insert all the pipes about 6 inches into their sleeves. Gradually work the fabric down over the pipes, bunching the material so both ends of the pipe stick out. Tie a very strong string onto the bottom of the left-end pipe. Then pull the string up tightly, insert it between the tops of the end pipe and the next pipe, pull it tightly down, and insert it between the bottoms of the same two pipes. Then repeat this step for the second and third pipes, pulling the string so it compresses the fabric between the pipes. Continue wrapping the string between each set of pipes, compressing the fabric as tightly as possible. Bind off at the other end (Figure 51).

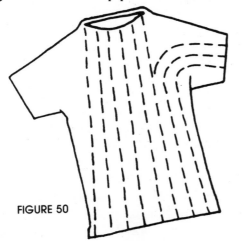

FIGURE 50

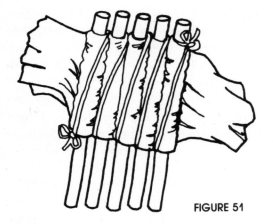

FIGURE 51

caused the fabric to shrink, so the pipes may be difficult to remove. The easiest way to wash the fabric is to cut off the binding string first and rinse the whole bundle, including the pipes. When the water is nearly clear, gradually ease the crushed fabric off the end of the pipes, continuing to rinse. When the water runs clear, do a soap soak and final rinsing. After the fabric is dry, use a seam ripper or small scissors to remove the stitches. (See Figure 52 for the completed shirt.)

Slide the fabric bundle to one end of the pipes, so it can be immersed in a dye bath. The plastic pipes as well as the crimping and binding will resist the dye. Stitching and crimping can also be used with direct-application and presoak dye techniques.

After the fabric has been dyed, it must be washed. The wetness of the dye process has

SPECIFIC-SHAPE PATTERNS

Using a cord to bind shaped areas of fabric before dyeing is a standard tie-dye technique. The areas that have been bound resist the dye and a specific pattern emerges. You can produce circles, squares, stripes, dots, and more.

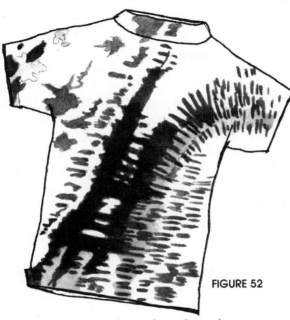

FIGURE 52

The binding cord needs only to be strong; it can be thick or thin. Binding cords could be cotton string, package cord, rubber bands, tire inner tubes cut into strips, plastic bags cut into strips, masking tape, elastic thread or ¼-inch elastic, linen, waxed linen, carpet thread, buttonhole twist, raffia, plastic box string from a grocery, Shibori tape, nylon fishing line, polypropylene binder twine, trash bag twist ties—just about anything you can imagine.

Thinner binding cord is necessary for finer fabrics. Coarser binding cord is necessary for greater tension, to cover larger areas more quickly, or to bind heavy fabrics. Finer threads will give thinner resist lines; coarse cords will give thick resist lines.

It is important that the binding thread not stretch or loosen in the dye bath. If that happens, the cord loses its ability to resist the dye. The binding should be as tight as possible without damaging the fabric.

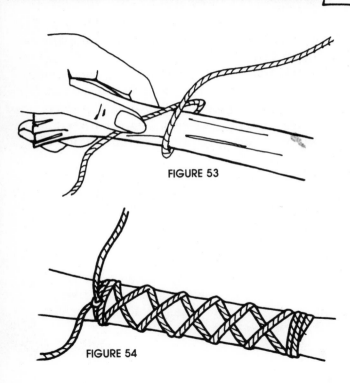

FIGURE 53

FIGURE 54

Secured knots

The binding cord should be securely knotted. The easiest method is to wrap the fabric bundle so the cord ends can be knotted together. Hold the bundle you want to tie in your left hand. Lay the binding cord on the bundle, leaving a 3-inch tail (Figure 53). Hold the tail under your left thumb. Wrap several times around the tail, just above your thumb. Continue to wrap diagonally up the bundle for the length you plan to bind, pulling tightly with each wrap. When you reach the upper limit of the resist area, wrap the cord around itself several times before diagonally wrapping back to where you began. Wrap around several times, then tie the two cord ends together securely in a square knot (Figure 54).

To tie very small points, use a needle and strong thread. Lay the washed and dried

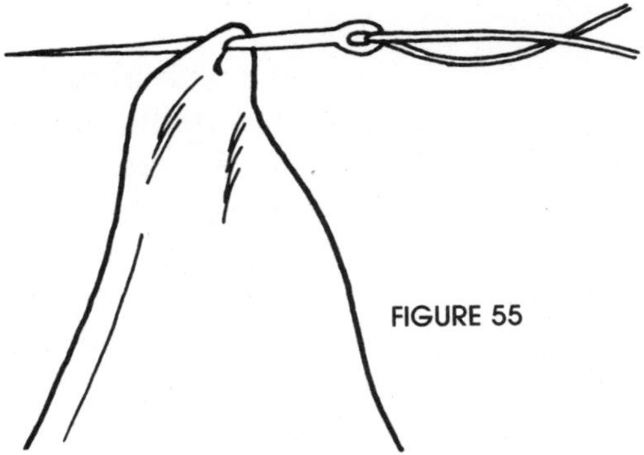

FIGURE 55

(Figure 56). Either stitch through the point three or four times to secure the wrapping, or tie an overhand knot with the tail. Without cutting the thread, proceed to the next point, repeating the process. Work in rows, so that as much knotting as possible can be done without cutting and restarting the thread.

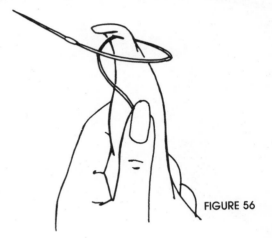

FIGURE 56

fabric out flat. Mark the points to be bound with a pencil or tailor's chalk. Using a threaded needle, pick up a marked point with the point of the needle (Figure 55). Smooth the fabric away from the needle; hold the fabric point in your left hand. Remove the needle from the fabric. Hold the tail of the thread under your left thumb. Wrap the point several times, pulling tightly as you wrap

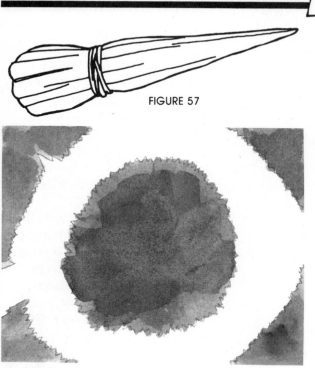

FIGURE 57

FIGURE 58

Circles, dots, and points

The easiest shape to make with binding is the circle. Pick up a point of fabric and smooth the fabric away from that point. The farther away from the point you bind (Figure 57), the larger the resisted circle (Figure 58). Concentric circles, or a bull's-eye, can be created by binding along the point at regular intervals (Figures 59 and 60).

Small circles, dots, and points can be created by placing small objects such as seeds, washers, stones, or pennies underneath the fabric. Grasp the object, wrapping the fabric over the object. Bind the fabric just below the object. The size of the object will determine the size of the circle. Oblong-shaped objects will make oval-shaped resists.

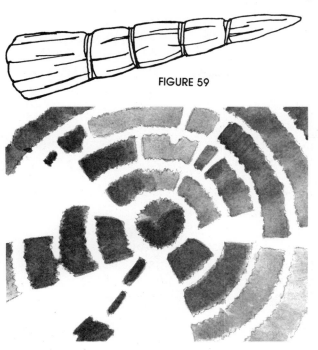

FIGURE 59

FIGURE 60

Stripes

Stripes are created by folding the fabric. Careful folds will make very regular stripes. Irregular folds make more organic stripes. The folded fabric can be bound with cord, twine, or rubber bands, or held in place with C-clamps. Each different binding will give a different pattern to the resist. The dye can be applied by the presoak, direct-application, or immersion methods.

The most obvious way to fold fabric is in accordion pleats. Various-size stripes can be created by folding the fabric in narrow pleats and binding the folded bundle at different intervals, leaving unbound areas between bindings (Figure 61). You will get stripes in two directions, one formed by the fold resist and the other formed by the binding resist (Figure 62).

FIGURE 61

Stripes of alternate colors can be made by accordion pleating the fabric using only enough bindings to hold the folds in place. One color of dye is applied to the folds on one side of the bundle and another color is applied to the folds on the other side of the

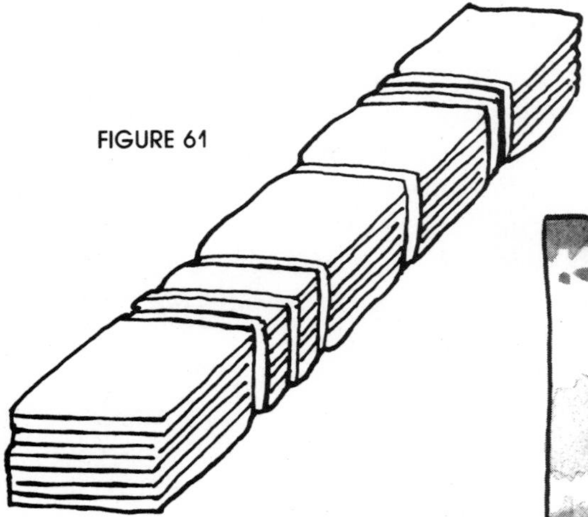

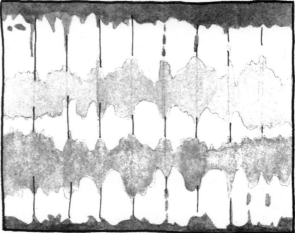

FIGURE 62

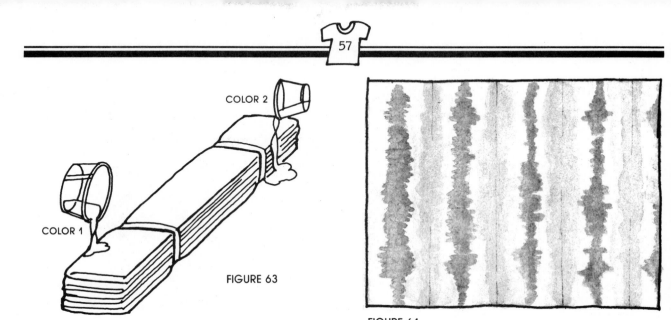

COLOR 2

COLOR 1

FIGURE 63

FIGURE 64

bundle (Figure 63). Shirt 1 uses this technique (Figure 64).

A "V" pattern can be made by first folding the fabric either on- or off-center. Then accordion fold at an angle anywhere from thirty degrees to seventy degrees from the center fold (Figure 65). This makes a long, thin bundle that is difficult to bind (Figure 66). Although it can be dyed using any of the methods, the presoak method works best

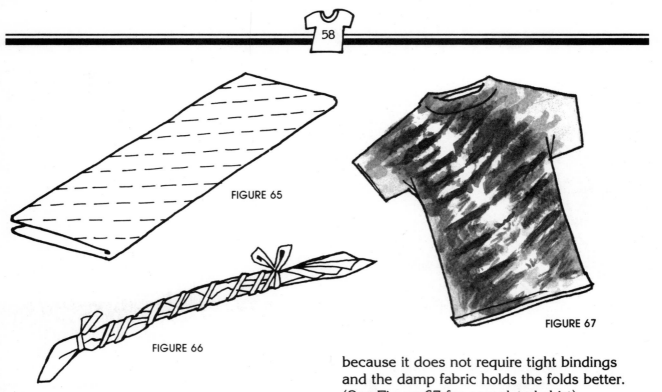

FIGURE 65

FIGURE 66

FIGURE 67

because it does not require tight bindings and the damp fabric holds the folds better. (See Figure 67 for completed shirt).

Squares

There are numerous ways to fold, bind, and dye squares, each resulting in different patterns. Many of the folds can be adapted to T-shirts. The most important aspect is to be accurate on the creasing to maintain the geometric shape.

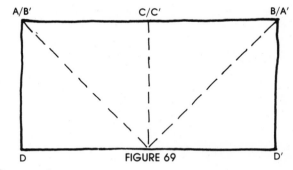

FIGURE 69

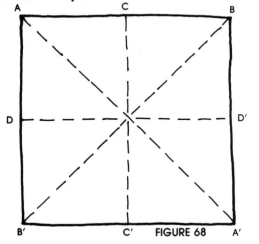

FIGURE 68

Square 1

Using a square piece of fabric (Figure 68), fold Point A to Point A′ and Point B to Point B′. Unfold. Fold Point C to Point C′ and Point D to Point D′. Unfold. Refold Point C to C′ (Figure 69) and tuck Points D and D′ inside to meet Point C/C′ (Figure 70). This makes a triangle. Accordion fold each of the wings from the line extending from the center point to Point C/C′ (Figure 71). Bind several times (Figure 72).

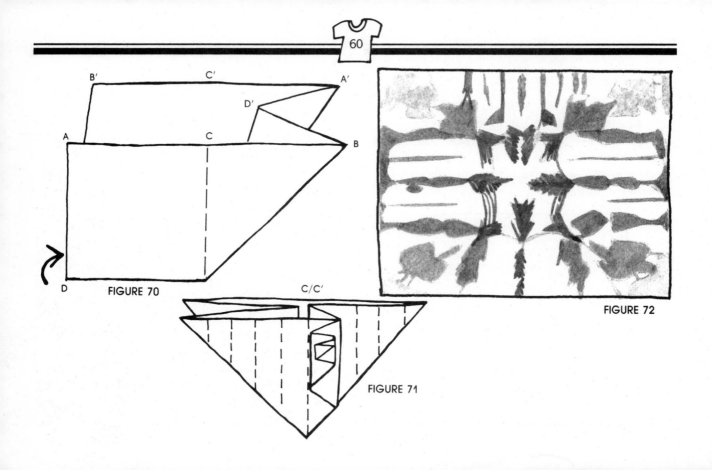

B' C' A'

D'

A C

B

D FIGURE 70

C/C'

FIGURE 71

FIGURE 72

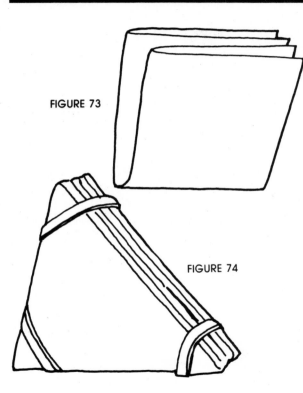

FIGURE 73

FIGURE 74

Square 2

Quarter-fold a square by folding a square in half, then in half again to make another square (Figure 73). Fold on the diagonal to make a triangle (Figure 74). Bind each of the points (Figure 75).

FIGURE 75

Square 3

Quarter-fold a square, as in Figure 73. Fold on the diagonal to make a triangle. Separate the points of the triangle by folding each point down, one forward, one backward (Figure 76). Bind (Figure 77).

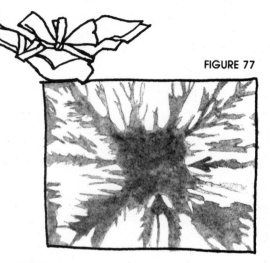

FIGURE 77

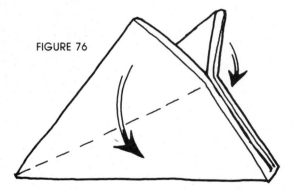

FIGURE 76

Square 4

Fold a square on the diagonal to make a triangle. Fold again to make a smaller triangle (Figure 78). Accordion fold from the base to the point (Figure 79). Bind (Figure 80).

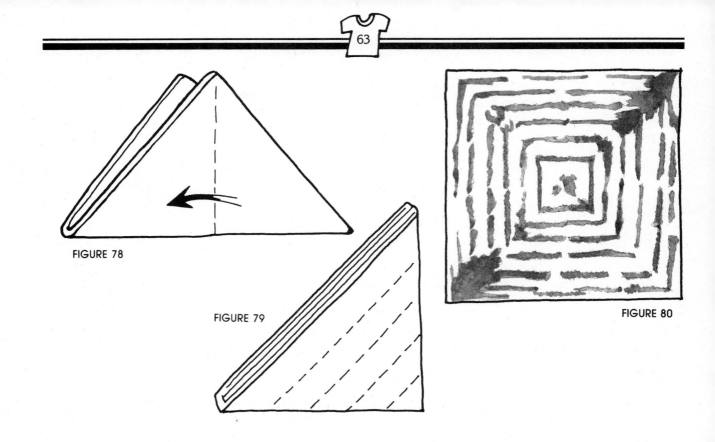

FIGURE 78

FIGURE 79

FIGURE 80

5
DYEING PAPER

Paper dyeing is an easy way to test patterns and create wrapping paper, book covers, note cards, etc. Folded patterns produce snowflake or kaleidoscope effects. Most of the patterns are quite simple folds; the patterns' complexities come from the application of dyes. These folding patterns can easily be adapted to use on fabrics.

Any dye can be used to dye paper, since light-fast and wash-fast properties are not required. Leftover dye from an immersion dye bath or direct-application dye to which fixer has been added can be used as well as fresh stock solution. Food coloring can be used and is especially suited for doing these projects with children.

Materials and equipment:

- Paper: Any light- to medium-weight porous paper that will not fall apart when wet. Grocery bags and brown wrapping paper are quite effective.
- Dye: Fiber-reactive dye mixed into stock solutions, or food coloring

- Tools: Paintbrushes, eyedroppers, syringes, and shallow pans for dipping
- Dish-washing gloves to protect hands
- Plastic drop cloth or plastic bags to cover work area
- Water in a small container for immersing the folded paper

Fold the paper in any of the following patterns. Quickly dip the folded packet in clear water to dampen the paper. This helps the dyes to spread, producing feathery edges to the color areas. Apply the dye by painting, dipping, or dripping it on the folded edges. When sufficient dye has been applied, set the folded paper bundle aside to dry. When it has dried to just slightly damp, unfold and lay the paper on a clean surface to dry flat. The paper can be ironed to remove creases.

FLAG FOLD

Fold a piece of paper in half lengthwise (Figure 81). Fold back one side on the quarter line and then the other side on the quarter line (Figure 82). The paper should look like a W.

Starting from one end (Figure 83), fold point A forward to meet point A^1 on line BC. Then fold point B backward on line CA^1, matching point B to point B^1. Fold forward on line CB^1, matching point A^1 to A^2. Continue in this manner until the whole paper is folded. Try to keep the fold lines as perfect as possible, creasing each line heavily.

Apply one color of dye to the points of the triangle and another color to the edges.

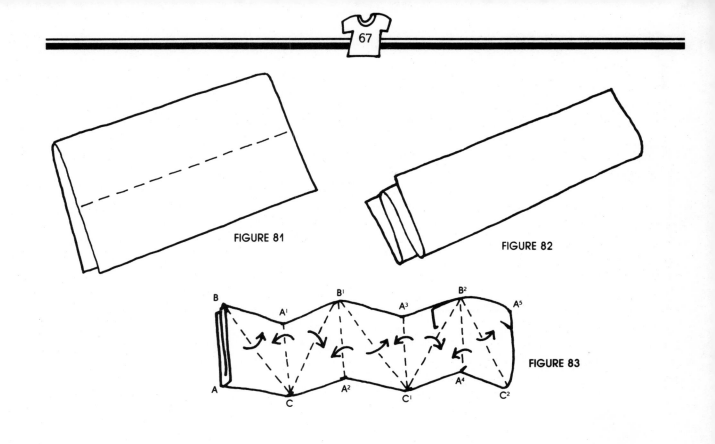

FIGURE 81

FIGURE 82

FIGURE 83

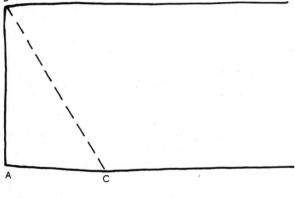

FIGURE 84

JAPANESE FOLD 1

Fold a piece of paper lengthwise into a W as in the Flag Fold. Measure the distance between points A and B (Figure 84). Divide that number by two for the distance between points A and C. Mark point C and line BC. Fold point A forward on line BC to point A' (Figure 85). Turn the paper over. Fold on line CD, matching the edge to line BC (Figure 86). Fold on line B'D, matching the edge to fold CD. Fold on line B'C', then C'D', continuing in this manner until the whole paper is folded into an equilateral triangle (Figure 87).

Apply different colors of dye to the edges and points.

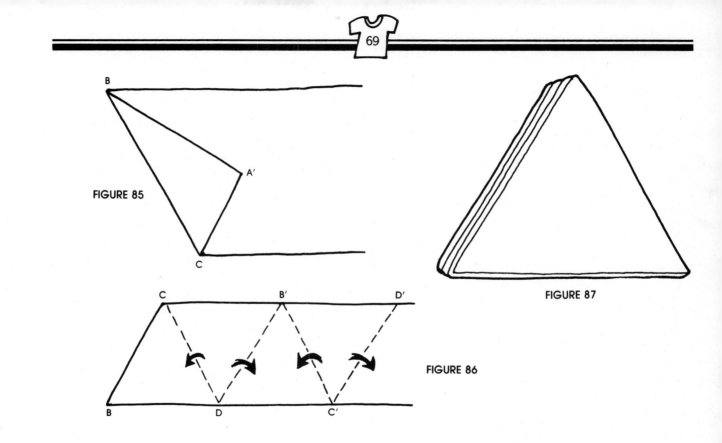

FIGURE 85

FIGURE 86

FIGURE 87

JAPANESE FOLD 2

Fold a piece of paper lengthwise into a W as in the Flag Fold. Starting from one end, fold point A forward on line BC to point A', which is halfway between C and C' (Figure 88). Angle ABC is a thirty-degree angle. Fold backward on line BD, matching point C to C' (Figure 89). Fold forward on line C^{1}D, matching point A to A^2 (Figure 90). Continue in this manner, folding backward and forward, matching the As, Bs, Cs, and Ds until the whole paper is folded into an isosceles triangle (Figure 91).

Apply dye along the folded edges.

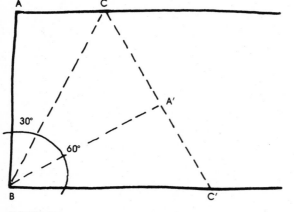

FIGURE 88

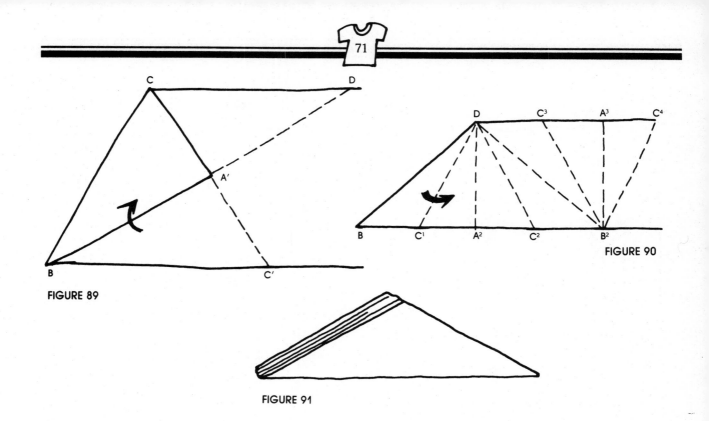

FIGURE 89

FIGURE 90

FIGURE 91

DOUBLE DIAGONAL FOLD

Starting from one corner, accordion fold a piece of paper on the diagonal in 1-inch folds (Figure 92). Fold the paper in half crosswise to create a line that is perpendicular to the accordion-fold lines (Figure 93). Unfold the paper (Figure 94). From the diagonal line, refold in 1-inch accordion folds, folding each half separately (Figure 95).

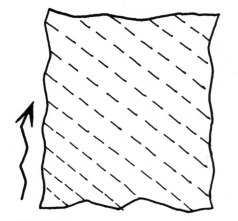

FIGURE 92

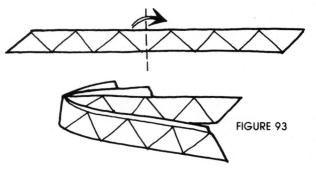

FIGURE 93

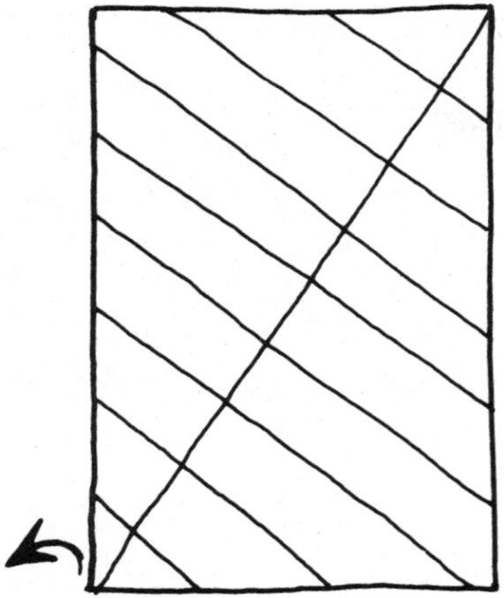

FIGURE 95

FIGURE 94

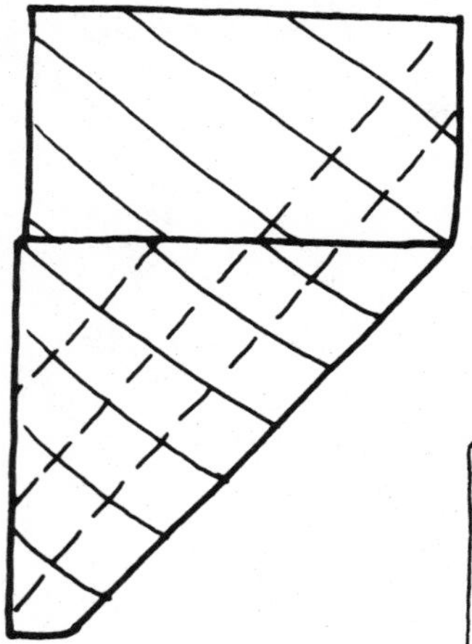

Accordion fold the resulting narrow band on the creases from the first folding. This makes a 1-inch square packet that can easily be dipped in dye. Apply dye to the edges only (Figure 96).

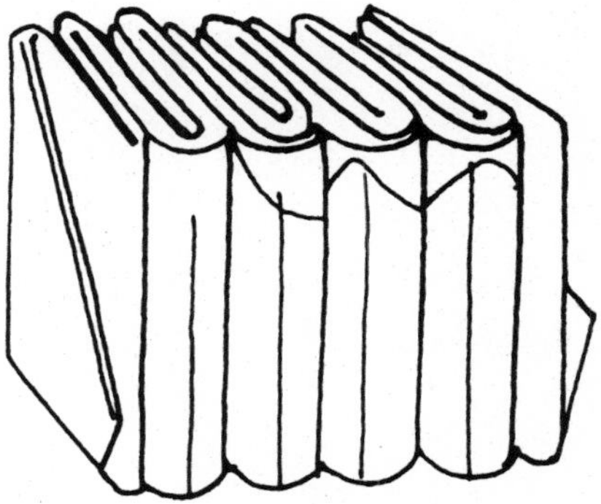

FIGURE 96

Let the bundle sit for 5 minutes so the dye can be absorbed. Unfold and refold on the other diagonal. Again, accordion fold the narrow band to make a 1-inch square packet. Dye these edges a different color. (See Figure 97 for completed paper.)

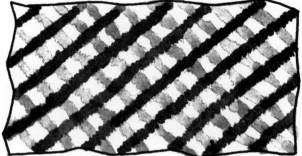

FIGURE 97

6
HALLOWEEN COSTUMES

Tie-dyeing Halloween costumes is a practical way to have unique yet utilitarian outfits for the chilly evening's hauntings. By using sweat suits or thermal long underwear, the costumes will be warm that evening and then can be transformed into pajamas for the winter.

Although difficult to find, 100 percent cotton fabrics are best because they dye much brighter. If you must use a blend, the cotton content should be at least half, such as 50 percent cotton-50 percent polyester or 50 percent cotton-50 percent acrylic. The higher the polyester or acrylic content, the paler the colors. Since the cotton content in sweat suits is often the fleece lining, wear the suit inside out for brighter colors and a more furlike appearance.

TIGER

Materials and Equipment:
• Sweatpants and sweatshirts or long underwear pants and shirt (yellow or white)

- A 5-inch-by-40-inch piece of cotton fabric for the tail
- Dishpan or dye bucket that will hold the outfit to be dyed
- 1-cup measuring cup, teaspoon, 2 jars for dye, stir spoons
- Dish-washing gloves
- Rubber bands or string for binding
- Syringe, ear syringe, pipette, or squeeze bottle for applying the dye
- Plastic drop cloth to cover work area
- Fiber-reactive dye: 4 teaspoons of black, 3 teaspoons of orange or gold-yellow
- ½ cup fixer (sodium carbonate) and 1½ cups salt
- Liquid dish-washing soap, 2 plastic bags

Procedure:

1. Wash new outfits to remove the sizing.

2. Fill the dishpan or dye bucket with 2½ gallons of water.

3. Add 1½ cups of salt. Stir.

4. In a separate cup, measure ½ cup of fixer. Add warm water. Stir with a spoon to dissolve. Pour the fixer solution into the presoak container. Stir.

5. Immerse the outfit to be dyed in the presoak solution for at least 30 minutes.

6. Prepare the dye stock solutions. Dissolve 4 teaspoons of black in 1½ cups of water and 3 teaspoons of orange or gold-yellow in 1½ cups of water (see pages 13-15). The black is mixed at a higher concentration because it is difficult to achieve a true black.

7. Wring out the shirt, pants, and tail so they are fairly damp.

8. Lay the pants flat on the work area; straighten the seams. Accordion fold each leg separately, starting from the bottom edge. Fold the leg at a 45-degree angle just above the cuff or hem, with the point of the angle on the outside seam (Figure 98). From that initial line, accordian fold 1- to 1½-inch pleats, on both sides of the line. Make the pleats inconsistent, varying the pleat sizes by ¼ to ½ inch (Figure 99). Using rubber bands or heavy string, bind the bundle every 5 inches (Figure 100). Continue folding the waist section at the angles of the legs. The waist area will have V stripes (Figure 101).

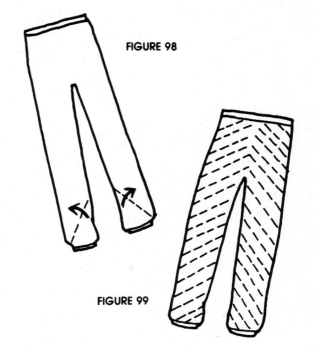

FIGURE 98

FIGURE 99

FIGURE 100

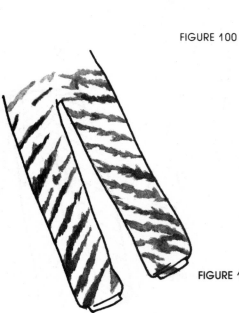

FIGURE 101

9. Lay the shirt flat on the work area; straighten the seams. Simultaneously fold the left and the right vertical halves of the shirt, starting from the lower corners of the body, at the hem or just above the ribbing. Accordion fold at a 45-degree angle to the center line of the shirt. Fold 1- to 1½-inch pleats. In the center of the shirt, press the fabric to the left or the right to keep the angles consistent. At the sleeves, continue folding at a 45-degree angle, making long folds (Figure 102). Bind the bundle every 5 inches with rubber bands or strong string (Figure 103). Fold the tail in a similar manner.

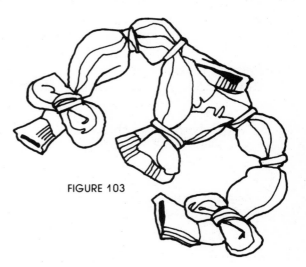

FIGURE 103

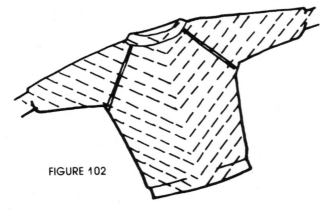

FIGURE 102

10. Squeeze the bundles to sharpen the pleats. This helps the dye permeate the fabric. Stand the bundles on their folded edges, so folds are on the top and bottom and the flat areas are on each side.

11. Using the syringe or other dye applicator, carefully apply black dye along each fold line on the top edges of the shirt, pants, and tail bundles. The dye should soak halfway down, about ½ to ¾ inch. Reserve about ¼ cup of the dye.

12. Turn the bundles over. Apply orange or gold-yellow dye along each fold line on the top of the bundles. Use all the dye. Squeeze the bundles to sharpen the pleats and force dye inside the pleats. Without removing the bindings, carefully open folds to see if the black dye permeated both layers. If not, insert the dye applicator into the fold and apply dye.

13. Place the bundles in plastic bags, black edges down, to await rinsing in 24 hours.

14. Wearing the dish-washing gloves, rinse each bundle separately, initially holding the black edges down so the black dye does not pollute the orange. Hold the bundle under warm running water, continually squeezing the bundle to remove excess dye. When the water is nearly clear, remove the bindings. Continue to rinse until the water runs clear.

15. Prepare a soap soak solution of ½ teaspoon liquid dish-washing soap to 2½

gallons of hot water. Immerse the rinsed garment for 5 to 10 minutes. Rinse the second garment and tail in the same manner. Continue to rinse in warm water and soap soak in hot water until the water runs clear. Up to five soap soaks may be necessary to remove all the excess dye.

16. Lay flat to dry.

17. Sew the tail into a long tube. Turn so the seam is on the inside. Stuff. Stitch or pin to the seat of the pants.

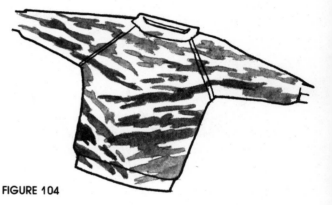

FIGURE 104

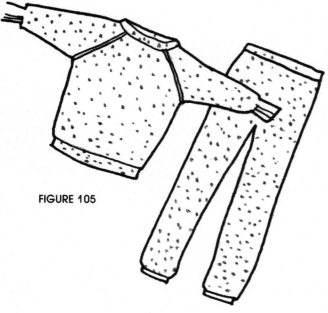

FIGURE 105

CHEETAH OR DALMATION

Materials and Equipment:

- White or yellow sweatpants and sweatshirt or long underwear pants and shirt, strip of fabric 5 inches by 40 inches for tail
- 1-cup measuring cup, measuring spoon, 1 jar for dye container
- Dish-washing gloves, dust mask
- 200 to 250 small rubber bands or a strong, fine binding cord
- Water spray bottle
- Small paintbrush or syringe for applying the dye
- Plastic drop cloth to cover the work area, several plastic garbage bags to insert inside the pants and shirt
- Fiber-reactive dye: 1 teaspoon black
- 4 teaspoons fixer (sodium carbonate)
- Liquid dish-washing soap, 2 plastic bags

Procedure:

1. Wash and dry outfit to remove sizing. The sizing keeps the dye from penetrating the fabric.

2. Lay the shirt and pants flat on the work area. Using a pencil, randomly mark points at approximately 1½- to 4-inch intervals all over each garment, front and back (Figure 105).

3. The front and back will be bound separately for better definition of color areas. The points are to be bound and dyed as small resist circles (see Chapter 4) to make the animal's spots. To bind a small circle, insert your hand inside the shirt or pants and push up a point of fabric. With the other hand, grasp the point. Smooth excess fabric away from the point to sharpen it. Grasp the fabric

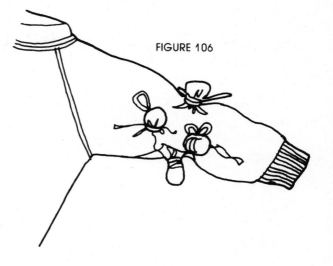

FIGURE 106

well below the point and bind ½ inch from the point. Bind all the points tightly (Figure 106). Binding 200 to 250 small circles will take several hours.

4. Prepare the dye stock solution by dissolving 1 teaspoon black dye in ½ cup water (see pages 13-15). Slowly add 4 teaspoons of fixer, stirring until completely dissolved.

5. Insert plastic bags inside the body, sleeves, legs, and trunk of the shirt and pants to prevent dye from soaking through to the other side.

6. Using water in a spray bottle, dampen the fabrics. Slightly damp fabric absorbs the dye more readily than dry fabric.

7. Using the brush or syringe, apply dye only to the small points. If the dye does not soak in easily, dampen the fabric again.

8. Place the shirt, pants, and tail in separate plastic bags to remain damp for 24 hours until rinsing.

9. Wearing the dish-washing gloves, remove the bindings before rinsing. Under warm tap water, rinse until the water runs clear and all the spots are free of excess dye. The background color may appear stained, but most of that dye will be drawn out in the soap soaks.

10. Prepare a soap solution with ½ teaspoon liquid dish-washing soap in 2½ gallons hot water. Immerse the garments for 5 to 10 minutes. Rinse again until the water runs clear. Continue to soap soak in hot

water and rinse in warm water until the background is clear and the rinse water is free of excess dye.

11. Lay flat to dry.

12. Sew the tail into a long tube. Turn so the seam is on the inside. Stuff. Sew or pin to the seat of the pants.

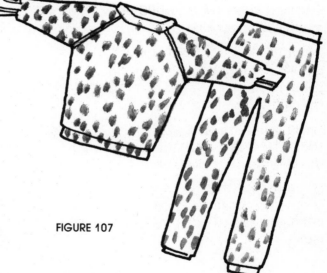

FIGURE 107

TIE-DYEING IN YOUR MICROWAVE

Fiber-reactive dyes fixed with white vinegar (mild acetic acid) can dye protein fibers such as silk and wool. Since protein fibers need to be heated for the dye to effectively bond with the material, the microwave is a convenient, rapid solution (and a fun alternative to conventional tie-dyeing, too). The microwave method can produce uneven coloration, which makes it perfect for multicolor tie-dyeing.

Materials and Equipment:
- One white or yellow silk or wool scarf, approximately 36" x 36"
- several colors of fiber-reactive dye, ⅛ to ¼ cup each
- dish-washing gloves
- quart-size wide-mouth jar or container
- distilled white vinegar, 5 percent concentration
- teaspoon-size measuring spoon
- needle and thread
- locking sandwich-size plastic bag
- paintbrush, syringe, or dye applicator

Procedure:
Fill the quart jar or container three-quarters full. Add 5 teaspoons vinegar if dyeing the silk scarf, 12 teaspoons if dyeing the wool scarf. Stir. Submerse the scarf, making sure it is completely below the surface. Allow the scarf to soak for 30 minutes.

Remove the scarf from the presoak solution. Squeeze out the excess water until slightly damp. Select one of the paper-folding patterns from Chapter 5 and carefully fold the scarf. If the bundle seems insecure, use several basting stitches through the whole bundle.

Wearing gloves, apply the dye generously to the scarf bundle. A star or snowflake design can be made by applying one color of dye to each of the corners. Apply a different color between the corners along the edges.

After all the dye has been applied, insert the scarf into the sandwich bag and lock. Place the bag in the microwave with the open edges of the bag down. Heat at full power for 2 minutes. The bag will expand, encasing the scarf in a steam bubble. To prevent the bag from exploding, stop the microwave after 45 seconds and 90 seconds, opening the door for 10 seconds to allow the bag to cool.

After 2 full minutes, remove the bag with a hot pad. When the scarf has cooled for 10 to 15 minutes, open the bag, remove the scarf, and take out the basting stitches. Rinse in running tap water, at approximately the same temperature as the scarf, until the water runs clear. Soak the scarf in a soap-water solution for 5 minutes; then rinse again until the water runs clear. Wring out excess water and lay flat to dry.

7
HOW TO THROW A
TIE-DYE PARTY

Tie-dye parties are grand events for all ages. The youngest participants I have hosted were four-year-olds. With younger children, have extra adult assistants to mix the dye and supervise. Have all participants bring two prewashed, 100 percent cotton T-shirts or sweatshirts. Tell each dyer to wear old clothes that can be thrown out if there are any accidents. Plan to work in a basement or outdoors.

Materials and Equipment:
- Plastic drop cloth to work on
- Buckets or dishpans for presoak
- Transparent plastic cups, cocktail-size because they do not tip easily
- One dye applicator per participant: syringes, squeeze bottles, ear syringes, etc.
- One pair of dish-washing or surgical gloves per participant

- Enough dye to make 1 cup of dye per participant, ½ cup dye per shirt
- 3 tablespoons fixer (sodium carbonate) per T-shirt
- Laundry marker to identify each shirt's owner
- Plastic bags to hold dyed shirts until rinsing, one per shirt
- Paper towels

Procedure:
Plan dye projects that will give dazzling results and be easily accomplished. Usually, for the first shirt, I help the dyers make shirt 1, the Diagonal Accordion Fold, presoak method. For younger children, I fold the shirts for them. Then, for the second shirt, they spread the shirt flat and draw on the shirt with the dyes, like Expressionist painters.

Measure dye powders and mix stock solutions (pages 13-15). Use 2 teaspoons of dye to 1 cup of water. Divide each cup of dye into 2 ½-cup portions. Prepare at least 1 cup of dye per person, mixing as many colors as possible because the dyers will want many options. Although ½ cup of dye for each shirt should be sufficient, the dyers will trade colors with each other and may be excessive with the dyes, so mix extra. Label each of the dye cups for color identification.

Prepare a presoak solution, dissolving 4 teaspoons of fixer and ¼ cup of salt per T-shirt or sweatshirt in sufficient water to cover the shirts.

Spread the drop cloth on a clean, level surface. Children prefer working on the ground or floor rather than on tables.

As each participant arrives, label each shirt on the tag with the dyer's initials or other identifying mark. Immerse the shirts in the presoak solution. All the shirts should presoak for at least 30 minutes for the best results.

Have the dyers gather around the drop cloth. Distribute cups of water and the dye applicators. Explain how to use the applicators and have the dyers practice with the water to gain expertise. Hand out the first shirts to be dyed and distribute the dyes and gloves. Encourage the dyers to share dye colors. Use the water cups to rinse out the dye applicators when changing colors.

After the first shirt is sufficiently dyed, place each shirt in a plastic bag until rinsing. Wipe off the work surfaces before placing the second shirt down. Apply the dye and place the second shirt in a plastic bag. You may decide to send the shirts home with the dyers for rinsing. If you do this, send specific instructions for successful rinsing.

Rinsing:
Keep the shirts damp for 24 hours before rinsing. Rinse each shirt individually until the water runs clear. Do a soap soak and rinse again. Lay shirts flat to dry (See pages 28-29).

APPENDIX A
WHAT YOU NEED TO
KNOW ABOUT
VARIOUS DYES

Dyes are defined and classified according to which fibers they can dye. There are many different classes of dye, each having its own, distinct chemical structure. Each dye class is specifically designed to effectively dye a particular type of fiber. The dye most suited for use on cotton and all natural fibers is fiber-reactive dye.

Fiber-reactive dyes first became available in 1956 under the trade name Procion. The dyes you received with this book are Dylon fiber-reactive dyes. Dylon fiber-reactive dyes are manufactured in England by International Chemical Industries under the name Procion. There are many manufacturers of fiber-reactive dyes. (See Appendix C for other dye suppliers.)

Fiber-reactive dyes require salt (table salt, iodized or noniodized salt) to encourage smooth, even take-up of the dye and a fixer (sodium carbonate, also known as sal soda, soda ash, or washing soda) to induce a chemical reaction between the dye and the fiber. This chemical bond permanently adheres the dye molecules to the fiber so the color is wash-fast and light-fast. If at all possible, you will want to work with the fiber-reactive dyes because they give the most flexibility when doing tie-dye. Fiber-reactive dyes often come prepackaged with the fixer. If a dye you are purchasing does not come with the fixer, read the instructions to see what, if any, chemicals are required. If no fixer is required, then the dye is not a fiber-reactive dye.

Fiber-reactive dyes will dye all natural fibers, that is, all fibers that occur in nature and are not man-made. This includes cotton, linen, wool, and silk. Cotton and linen are plant, or cellulose, fibers. Wool and silk are animal, or protein, fibers. Fiber-reactive dyes will also dye rayon, a fiber made from regenerated cellulose. Fiber-reactive dyes will *not* dye other man-made fibers, such as polyester, acrylic, dacron, and fortrel because these fibers are petrochemical derivatives.

APPENDIX B
TROUBLESHOOTING
YOUR TIE-DYE

If I cannot find fiber-reactive dyes, can I use Rit or Cushing dye for tie-dye?

Rit and Cushing dyes are household dyes, available at groceries, fabric and craft stores, and drugstores. It is necessary for these dyes to be applied in a hot immersion-type dye bath for the dye to be effective. They will not work for presoak or direct-application methods, so multicolor tie-dye is not possible.

The background color is dingy and did not remain bright. What can I do?

If you have already dried your garment, there is nothing that can be done. The excess dye has probably bonded to the fiber or at least stained it. If you are still rinsing, continue to soap soak and rinse. If the fabric is thick, it may take between 5 and 10 soap soaks to really remove all the excess dye.

What liquid soap should I use?

Although there are soaps specifically prepared for dyes available from the dye suppliers, dish-washing liquids such as Ivory that are mild detergents *without* whiteners and brighteners are quite satisfactory.

I know I should always wear gloves when dyeing, but I didn't. How do I remove the stains?

Many of the dye suppliers sell hand cleaner that is quite effective and nontoxic. If you do not have any, use Lava soap and a fingernail brush and scrub. Do not use bleach since it can be hazardous.

The pattern I bound did not appear. What happened?

Your binding was not tight enough. The binding needs to be so tight that it must either be cut or completely untied to remove it. Often tie-dyers will tape their hands in order to pull the bindings tight without getting blisters.

How do I wash tie-dyed garments?

Machine wash in cool water, either separately or with other garments that will not be damaged if there is still any excess dye. Usually after two machine washings, all excess dye is completely removed.

Why can't I use the washing soda from the laundry section of the grocery store as fixer?

The laundry version of washing soda has perfumes and brighteners that disrupt the chemical reaction of the dye. The colors will be splotchy, uneven, and pale. Purchase sodium carbonate (sal soda or soda ash) from swimming pool chemical suppliers. Sodium bicarbonate (baking soda) is not the same and will not work with the dyes.

I have a piece of red cotton fabric. Can I tie-dye it?

Dyes are like transparent washes in water color—the color is additive. If your fabric is any color, the dye added will alter the color but cannot completely change it. For example, if the fabric is red, by dyeing it blue the new color will be purple, the sum of red and blue. The fabric cannot become blue. Yellow dye is relatively weak and cannot alter dark colors. Yellow over red will only slightly change the red; but red over yellow will easily make orange. Dark blues, purples, and browns can be overdyed only with strong colors like red, navy blue, or black. Other color cannot change dark colors significantly.

Where can I buy dye applicators?

Ear syringes, medicine syringes for babies, and other syringes can be found in drugstores. Used contact lens solution bottles, nasal spray squeeze bottles, and similar bottles work well also. Farm and veterinary supply stores carry animal syringes in larger sizes.

When I rinse, there seems to be a lot of dye going down the drain. Am I wasting dye or washing it off the fabric?

Not all of the dye molecules will bond to the fibers. Many of the molecules will bond to the hydrogen molecules in the water. Only a certain quantity will ever truly bond to the fibers, so there always will be excess dye.

APPENDIX C
FINDING SUPPLIES FOR
MORE DYEING

Ready for more dye projects? You can purchase additional dye from your local yarn store or craft shop. Be sure to purchase *fiber-reactive dyes*. If you are not certain that the dye is a fiber-reactive dye, read the instructions. If the instructions call for washing soda, sodium carbonate, or fixer and the dye bath can be run at room temperature, then it is probably a fiber-reactive dye. Other kinds of dye will require heat or the addition of some form of acid (acetic acid, vinegar, sulphuric acid). These

dyes are not suitable for this form of tie-dye. The suppliers may also carry liquid fiber-reactive dyes, which are a convenient yet slightly more expensive form of fiber-reactive dye. Consult Appendix A for further information on fiber-reactive dyes.

The fixer, sodium carbonate, is different from baking soda, sodium bicarbonate. Baking soda will not work with fiber-reactive dyes for tie-dye. Sodium carbonate can be purchased from your dye suppliers or from swimming pool chemical suppliers. It is sold under the name *soda ash* or *sal soda* in 1-pound packages. Occasionally water softening companies will stock sodium carbonate.

Canning or pickling salt is the least expensive form of salt to use, because it is available in 5- or 10-pound packages. You can use either iodized or noniodized salt.

FIBER-REACTIVE DYE SUPPLIERS

Keep in mind that you are handling industrial chemicals when you use dyes. You should use dyes in a responsible manner to protect yourself, those around you, and your environment. The following companies sell fiber-reactive dyes, safety equipment, books, and measuring equipment:

Brooks & Flynn
Box 2639
Rohnert Park, CA 94927

Cerulean Blue, Ltd.
P.O. Box 21168
Seattle, WA 98111-3168
   Cibacron F and Procion Fiber-Reactive Dye

Createx Colors
Division of Color Craft Ltd.
14 Airport Park Road
East Granby, CT 06026
   Createx Liquid Fiber-Reactive Dye

Dharma Trading Co.
P.O. Box 916
San Rafael, CA 94915
   Dyehouse Procion Fiber-Reactive Dye

Earth Guild
One Tingle Alley
Asheville, NC 28801

FabDec
3553 Old Post Road
San Angelo, TX 76904
　Procion Fiber-Reactive Dye

Farquhar International Limited
56 Harvester Avenue
Batavia, NY 14020
　Dylon Cold-Water Dye

Keystone Aniline & Chemical Co.
2501 W. Fulton
Chicago, IL 60612

PRO Chemical & Dye
P.O. Box 14
Somerset, MA 02726
　Cibacron F and Pro Fiber-Reactive Dye

Textile Resources
P.O. Box 90245
Long Beach, CA 90809

BIBLIOGRAPHY

DYEING

Blumenthal, Betsy, and Kathryn Kreider. *Hands-on Dyeing*. (Loveland, CO: Interweave Press, 1988).

Granich, Ronald B. *Japanese Paste-Resist Dyeing*. (Seattle: Cerulean Blue Ltd., 1979).

Johnson, Meda Parker, and Glen Kaufman. *Design on Fabric*. (New York: Van Nostrand Reinhold, 1967).

Knutson, Linda. *Synthetic Dyes for Natural Fibers*. (Loveland, CO: Interweave Press, 1986).

Larsen, Jack Lenor. *The Dyers Art: Ikat, Batik, Planqi*. (New York: Van Nostrand Reinhold, 1976).

Maille, Anne. *Tie-Dye as a Present-Day Craft*. (London: Mills and Boon Ltd., 1969).

Meilach, Dona Z. *Contemporary Batik & Tie-Dye*. (New York: Crown Publishers, 1973).

Proctor, Richard M., and Jennifer F. Lew. *Surface Design for Fabric.* (Seattle: University of Washington Press, 1984).

Robinson, Stuart. *A History of Dyed Textiles.* (Cambridge, MA: M.I.T. Press, 1969).

Storey, Joyce. *The Thames and Hudson Manual of Dyes and Fabrics.* (London: Thames and Hudson Publishers, 1978).

Trotman, E. R. *Dyeing and Chemical Technology of Textile Fibers.* (London: Charles Griffin, 1975).

Vinroot, Sally, and Jennie Crowder. *The New Dyer.* (Loveland, CO: Interweave Press, 1981).

Wada, Yoshiko. *Shibori: The Inventive Art of Japanese Shaped Resist Dyeing.* (Tokyo: Kodansha, 1983).

COLOR

Albers, Josef. *Interaction of Color.* (New Haven, CT: Yale University Press, 1975).

Allen, Jeanne. *Showing Your Colors.* (San Francisco: Chronicle Books, 1986).

——. *Designer's Guide to Color Three.* (San Francisco: Chronicle Books, 1986).

Itten, Johannes. Edited by Faber Birren. *The Elements of Color.* (New York: Van Nostrand Reinhold, 1970).

Stockton, James. *Designer's Guide to Color 1 and 2.* (San Francisco: Chronicle Books, 1984).

Wong, Wucius. *Principles of Color Design.* (New York: Van Nostrand Reinhold, 1986).

PERIODICALS

Surface Design Journal. 4111 Lincoln Boulevard, Suite 426, Marina Del Rey, CA 90292. Magazine for dyers, surface designers.

Threads. The Taunton Press, P.O. Box 355, Newtown, CT 06470. Magazine for entire range of fiber arts.